# English Grammar Taught with Help from Stanford

Melanie Richardson Dundy

Copyright © 2019 Melanie Richardson Dundy

ISBN: 978-0-578-54088-7

All rights reserved.
No part of this book may be reproduced without
express written permission from the author.

Printed in the United States of America

**MDCT Publishing**
melanie.dundy@icloud.com
website: ChildrensBooksByMelanie.com

*For my father who insisted I know the difference between who and whom, as well as other basic grammar, at a very young age. His encouragement made my life easier from grade school through college and beyond. I learned to love the nuances of the English language.*

*Thanks Dad.*

# Table of Contents

Note to Teachers, Parents, and Students
Introduction to Stanford
Power of Words

| | |
|---|---|
| **Chapter 1: Sentences** | 1 |
| simple/declarative sentence | 4 |
| compound sentence | 5 |
| complex sentence | 7 |
| comma and the complex sentence | 9 |
| interrogative sentence | 11 |
| imperative sentence | 12 |
| run-on sentence | 13 |
| **Chapter 2: Eight Parts of Speech** | 15 |
| noun | 16 |
| singular noun, plural noun | 17 |
| collective noun | 21 |
| possessive noun | 22 |
| pronoun | 23 |
| personal pronoun | 24 |
| possessive pronoun | 25 |
| demonstrative pronoun | 26 |
| interrogative pronoun | 27 |
| indefinite pronoun | 28 |
| relative pronoun | 29 |
| adjective | 31 |
| verb | 32 |
| helping/auxiliary verb | 33 |
| linking verb | 34 |
| predicate nominative | 36 |
| predicate adjective | 37 |

| | |
|---|---|
| adverb | 38 |
| preposition | 40 |
| conjunction | 42 |
|    coordinating conjunctions | 43 |
|    subordinate conjunctions | 44 |
|    paired conjunctions | 45 |
| interjection | 46 |
| article (indefinite/definite) | 47 |

## Chapter 3: Punctuation — 53

| | |
|---|---|
| period | 54 |
| question mark | 55 |
| exclamation point | 56 |
| quotation marks | 57 |
|    periods/commas with quotation marks | 59 |
|    question marks/exclamation points with quotation marks | 60 |
| comma | 61 |
| apostrophe | 62 |
|    with contractions | 63 |
|    with singular possessive nouns | 64 |
|    with plural possessive nouns | 66 |

## Chapter 4: Subject and Verb Agreement — 67

## Chapter 5: Capitalization — 73

## Chapter 6: Syllables — 79

## Chapter 7: Words and More Words — 83

| | |
|---|---|
| compound words | 84 |
| contractions | 86 |
| words easily confused | 88 |
|    accept, except | 89 |
|    advice, advise | 90 |
|    affect, effect | 91 |
|    already, all ready | 92 |
|    anyone, any one | 93 |
|    anyway, any way | 94 |
|    conscious, conscience | 95 |

| | |
|---|---|
| everyday, every day | 96 |
| hear, listen | 98 |
| its, it's | 99 |
| lay, lie | 100 |
| lead, led | 101 |
| like, as | 102 |
| look, watch, see | 103 |
| maybe, may be | 104 |
| than, then | 105 |
| their, there, they're | 106 |
| to, too, two | 107 |
| were, we're | 108 |
| who, whom | 109 |
| your, you're | 111 |
| synonyms/antonyms | 112 |
| palindromes/anagrams | 115 |
| words with silent letters | 118 |
| onomatopoeias | 121 |
| oxymorons | 125 |
| short words/long words | 127 |
| **Chapter 8: Grammar NO NOs** | **131** |
| **Final Note from Stanford** | **134** |

Note to teachers, parents, and students —

This is the book I wish I had written for my son when he was struggling to learn the ins and outs of English grammar. I would like to think my early tutoring in grammar and writing was at least partly responsible for him later acquiring a degree in journalism.

Even though a strong foundation in English grammar remains an essential element for success in social, academic, and business environments, the proper use of grammar is getting lost in our world of messsaging and texting. Without a solid knowledge of English grammar, opportunities offered and success experenced in almost any endeaver may be limited.

This book is a one-stop reference with a simple, quick, easy to understand, no nonsense approach to everyday grammar and punctuation questions.

Check out the Table of Contents to see if this is the book you need. I hope it is.

Melanie Richardson Dundy

Even though our alphabet is made up of only 26 letters, there are over one million words in the English language.

So, how can 1,000,000 words be made out of only 26 letters?

Letters are put together
in many different ways
to make many different words
that mean many different things
to many different people
in many different situations.
Whew!!

People will judge you throughout your life by the way you use words in speech and writing. That might not seem fair, but it is the truth.

Words are our means of communicating. They can do a lot of good or a lot of harm depending on who is using them, how they are being used, and what is being said.

Words can start wars, bring peace, initiate respect, cause hurt feelings, create trust, instill confidence, and contribute to the success or failure of everything we attempt in life.

Words teach, describe, entertain, depress, soothe, harm, comfort, explain, inform, misinform, motivate, relieve, compliment, console, excite, communicate, encourage, discourage, invigorate, humiliate, educate, descipline, compare, and so much more.

# Now that's power!

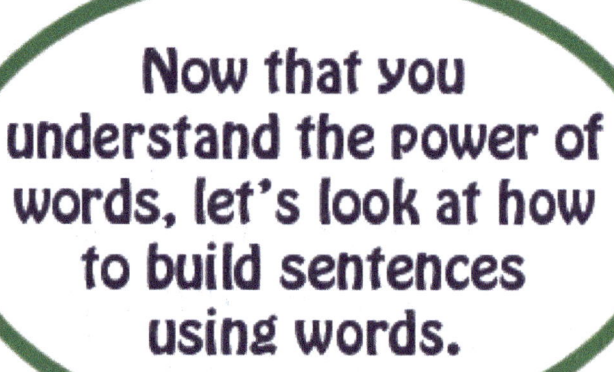

## Chapter 1: Sentences

***A sentence is a group of words that expresses a complete thought.***

A sentence begins with a capital letter.

A sentence ends with a period, question mark, or exclamation point.

A sentence has a subject and a verb.

The subject is the part of the sentence that is doing something.

The verb describes the action in a sentence. It tells us what the subject is doing.

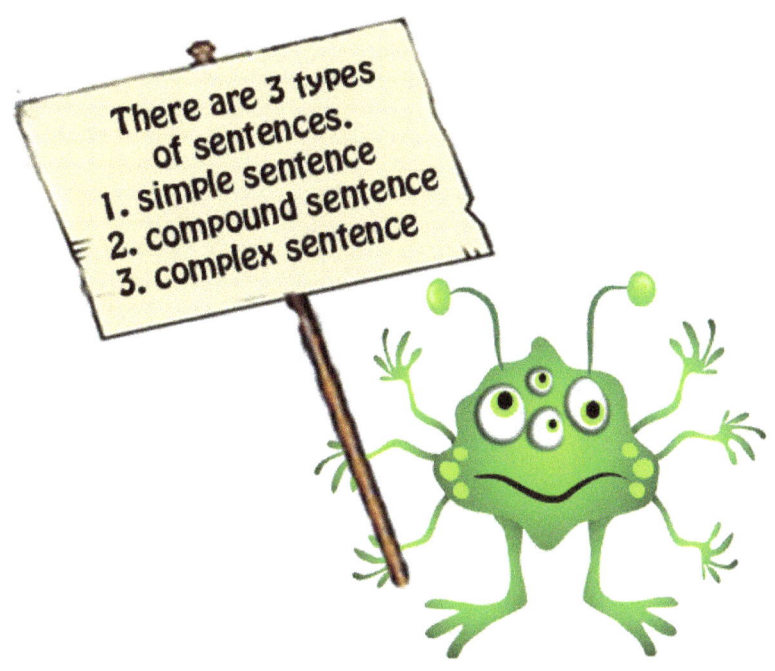

All sentences are made up of one or more clauses, and each clause contains a subject and a verb.

There are only 2 types of clauses for you to learn, and they are not hard to understand.

1. An **independent clause**, also called *a main clause*, is a group of words that form a **complete thought**.

>An independent clause can stand alone as a sentence.

2. A **dependent clause**, also called a *subordinate clause*, is a group of words that is **not a complete thought**.

>A dependent clause is an incomplete thought that cannot stand alone as a sentence.

## SIMPLE or DECLARATIVE SENTENCE

A *simple sentence* is *one independent clause.*
(one complete thought with a subject and a verb)

    The clouds are thick.
    (*clouds* is the subject, *are* is the verb)

    She hopes it is true.
    (*She* is the subject, *hopes* is the verb)

    The dog ran away.
    (*dog* is the subject, *ran* is the verb)

## COMPOUND SENTENCE

A compound sentence is two or more independent or main clauses (two or more complete thoughts) separated by a comma and joined by a coordinating conjunction.

A coordinating conjunction - and, but, for, nor, yet, or, so - connects the two independent clauses in a compound sentence. (Coordinating conjunctions are covered in Chapter 2.)

The clauses in a compound sentence are equal, and each clause can stand alone as a complete sentence.

I like rain, but I don't like snow.

He smiled at me, and I began to giggle.

The snow kept falling, but the roof did not collapse.

# More Examples of Compound Sentences

He ate his lunch, and he fed the dog.

**He ate his lunch** and **he fed the dog** are independent clauses. Each can stand alone as a sentence.

She kicked the ball well, and she made a goal.

**She kicked the ball well** and **she made a goal** are independent clauses. Each can stand alone as a complete sentence.

She studied hard, so she got good grades.

**She studied hard** and **she got good grades** are independent clauses. Each can stand alone as a sentence.

Jim fell down, and he got a bruise.

**Jim fell down** and **he got a bruise** are independent clauses. Each can stand alone as a sentence.

## COMPLEX SENTENCE or CONDITIONAL SENTENCE

A complex sentence is *a main clause* (complete thought) connected by a subordinate conjunction to one or more *dependent clauses* (incomplete thought or thoughts).

Common subordinate conjunctions used in complex sentences are:

> after, as, as if, as soon as, as long as, before, because, during, even though, if, since, though, until, unless, where, and, wherever, while, when, whenever

Subordinate conjunctions are covered more fully in Chapter 2.

*(Examples of complex sentences on next page)*

## Examples of Complex Sentences

Had he worked harder, he would have passed the test.

The main, or independent clause, is **he would have passed the test**. It can stand alone as a complete sentence. **Had he worked harder** is the dependent clause. It cannot stand alone as a sentence.

We went to the store before it closed.

**We went to the store** is the main clause. It can stand alone as a sentence. The dependent clause is **before it closed**. It is not a complete thought.

Unless you listen, you will not learn.

The main clause is **you will not learn**. It is a complete thought that can stand alone as a sentence. **Unless you listen** is the dependent clause. It is not a complete thought and cannot stand alone as a sentence.

## the comma and the complex sentence

*Use a comma [ , ] to sepaarate an introductory dependent (cannot stand alone) clause from an independent (can stand alone) clause.*

*examples:*

When he cleaned up the spilled milk, he forgot to put the cereal away.

**When he cleaned up the spilled milk** is an *introductory dependent clause* because (a) it comes at the beginning of the sentence - introduces the sentence, and (b) it cannot stand alone making it dependent on the rest of the sentence to make sense.

The *independent clause* is **he forgot to put the cereal away**. It can stand alone as a complete sentence. A comma is used to separate the clauses.

After he finished his homework, he climbed a tree.

**After he finished his homework** is an *introductory clause* because it introduces the sentence. It is a dependent clause because it cannot stand alone.

The *independent clause* is **he climbed a tree**. It is a complete thought that can stand alone as a sentence. A comma is used to separate the clauses.

## BUT . . .

**BUT . . .**

In a complex sentence, DO NOT use a comma [ , ] to separate an introductory independent (can stand alone) clause from a dependent (cannot stand alone) clause.

*examples:*

Juan visited the zoo before feeding time.

***Juan visited the zoo*** is the *introductory clause*. It introduces the sentence. It is an *independent clause* that can stand alone.

The *dependent clause* is **before feeding time**. It cannot stand alone and comes at the end of the sentence. Do not use a comma between the introductory independent clause and the dependent clause.

We will be studying unless tomorrow's test is postponed.

***We will be studying*** introduces the sentence, so it is an introductory clause. It is an *independent clause* that can stand alone as a sentence.

The dependent clause, **unless tomorrow's test is postponed,** cannot stand alone, so no comma is necessary.

## *INTERROGATIVE SENTENCE*

***An interrogative sentence asks a question and ends with a question mark.***

Interrogative sentences frequently start with *who, what, where, when,* or *why.*

*examples:*

> *Who* is that standing next to your dad?
>
> *What* are you doing?
>
> *Where* are you?
>
> *When* will you be home?
>
> *Why* would you want to be his friend?

Interrogative sentences can be constructed as simple, complex, or compound sentences.

> How old are you?
> (simple interrogative sentence)
>
> If I told you I was old, would you believe me?
> (complex interrogative sentence)
>
> Who are you, and what are you doing here?
> (compound interrogative sentence)

## IMPERATIVE SENTENCE

**An imperative sentence is a command.**

The implied subject in an imperative sentence is <u>**you**</u>.

Imperative sentences are often followed by an exclamation point.

*examples:*

> Come here!
>
> Do not forget to wash your hands.
>
> Do not eat anything that will spoil your dinner.
>
> Cover your mouth when you sneeze!
>
> Tell me the truth now!

Imperative sentences can be constructed as simple, complex, or compound sentences.

> Come here!
> (simple imperative sentence)
>
> When I call, you come here!
> (complex imperative sentence)
>
> Listen to me, and come when I call!
> (compound imperative sentence)

## RUN-ON SENTENCE

***A run-on sentence is NOT a good thing.***

Run-on sentences have little or no punctuation. Lack of punctuation makes a sentence difficult to understand.

***Check out this example of a run-on sentence.***

**Dad worked all day he is very tired.**

*Solution #1*

Correct the run-on sentence by using a period to make it into two sentences. Two sentences are easier to understand than one run-on sentence.

**Dad worked all day. He is very tired.**

*Solution #2*

Correct the run-on sentence by making it a compound sentence using a comma and a conjunction.

**Dad worked all day, and he is very tired.**

*Solution #3*

Correct the run-on sentence by making it a complex sentence with an introductory dependent (cannot stand alone) clause.

**Because dad worked all day, he is very tired.**

## Chapter 2: Eight Parts of Speech

***Parts of speech are divided into eight categories.***

1. **Noun** (person, place, or thing)
2. **Pronoun** (word that can replace a noun)
3. **Verb** (action word - something is happening)
4. **Adjective** (describes a noun or pronoun)
5. **Adverb** (answers questions, how? where? when? to what extent?) Adverbs often end in "ly."
6. **Preposition** (describes the relationship between words in a sentence)
7. **Conjunction** (connects/joins parts of a sentence)
8. **Interjection** (expresses sudden emotion) Interjections are often followed by exclamation points.

## NOUN

**A noun is a person, place, or thing.**

| | |
|---|---|
| person | (boy, girl, neighbor, teacher) |
| place | (home, restaurant, mall, school) |
| thing | (ball, television, kite, doll, bug) |

**A proper noun is a SPECIFIC person, place, or thing and is capitalized.**

specific person (Sue, Harry Potter, Spiderman)

specific place   (Los Angeles, Africa, Disneyland)

specific thing   (Lincoln Memorial, Civil War, Kleenex)

## singular nouns, plural nouns

***A singular noun is one person, one place, or one thing.***

girl

playground

worm

***A plural noun is more than one person, place, or thing.***
To make most nouns plural, simply add the letter "s" to the singular noun.

girls

playgrounds

worms

Just adding an "s" is easy to remember, right? It is a little too easy. You probably already have the feeling in the pit of your stomach that there are exceptions to this rule. Sadly, you are right. Stanford will explain the exceptions on the next page, but I guarantee you will not like them.

## rules for making nouns plural

**1. Singular nouns that end in — s, ss, ch, sh, x — need an "es" added to make them plural.**

> bus (buses)
> guess (guesses)
> witch (witches)
> bush (bushes)
> box (boxes)

**2. Some singular nouns have to be spelled in a totally different way to make them plural.**
These are the difficult ones, because you have to memorize them.

> goose (geese)
> child (children)
> man (men)
> person (people)
> woman (women)
> mouse (mice)
> louse (lice)
> fungus (fungi)

**3. Some nouns are spelled the same whether singular or plural.**

> deer (deer)
> moose (moose)
> fish (fish)
> pants (pants)
> shorts (shorts)
> scissors (scissors)

**4. Making words that end in "y" plural is tricky unless you remember the following two things.**

If the letter before the "y" is a vowel (a, e, i, o, u), just add "s."

> more than one galley (galleys)
>
> more than one day (days)
>
> more than one killjoy (killjoys)

If the letter before the "y" is a consonant (any letter other than a vowel), change the "y" to "i" and add "es".

> more than one baby (babies)
>
> more than one lady (ladies)
>
> more than one berry (berries)
>
> more than one butterfly (butterflies)

**5. To make words that end in "f" or "fe" plural, change the "f" or "fe" to a "v" followed by "es."**

    more than one knife (knives)

    more than one leaf (leaves)

    more than one hoof (hooves)

    more than one life (lives)

    more than one self (selves)

    more than one elf (elves)

## collective noun

***A collective noun refers to a group of people, animals, ideas, or objects as a single thing.***

There are close to 200 collective nouns in the English language. Almost all of them can be replaced with the word "group."

*army* of ants
*deck* of cards
*group* of children
*class* of students
*jury* of peers
*majority* of people
*board* of directors
*pride* of lions
*murder* of crows
*pack* of wolves
*herd* of elephants
*box* of crayons
*pad* of paper
*bouquet* of flowers
*team* of players
*gaggle* of geese

### Matching the verb to the collective noun

A *collective noun* is followed by a *singular verb*.

The pride of lions *is* attacking.
The deck of cards *has* been dealt.
The group of ideas *is* impressive.
The bouquet of flowers was romantic.

possessive noun

**A *possessive noun* shows ownership.**

An apostrophe [ ' ] is used to create a possessive noun. Possessive nouns tell us what belongs to whom.

This is Stanford's dog.

*(Possessive nouns with apostrophes are covered in more detail in Chapter 3.)*

## PRONOUN

**A pronoun is a word that can take the place of a noun.**

*He, she, you, I, me, they, we,* and *it* are all pronouns that can replace nouns in a sentence.

There are seven categories of pronouns.

        Subjective Pronouns

        Objective Pronouns

        Possessive Pronouns

        Demonstrative Pronouns

        Interrogative Pronouns

        Indefinite Pronouns

        Relative Pronouns

All of them will be covered in the following pages.

## personal pronoun

***A personal pronoun takes the place of a person's name.***

In the sentence, *Susan went to the movies*, "***she***" can replace Susan. Therefore, ***she*** is a personal pronoun.

There are two types of personal pronouns.

1. A ***subjective personal pronoun*** is used as the subject of a sentence (the person doing something or being something).

| | |
|---|---|
| I | (I plan to win the race.) |
| you | (You were right all along.) |
| he, she, it | (He said I could have the book.) |
| we | (We plan to see that movie later.) |
| you | (You are the best friend I ever had.) |
| they | (They said I was smart.) |

2. An ***objective personal pronoun*** is the object of a sentence (the person receiving the action).

| | |
|---|---|
| me | (Hand me the list of names.) |
| you | (I ask you not to tell anyone.) |
| him, her, it | (Kim told her to wait outside.) |
| us | (Mom gave us a present.) |
| them | (Charlie wants them to go home.) |

### possessive pronoun

***A possessive pronoun is used to show possession or ownership .***

You will always find possessive pronouns in the object (receiver) of a sentence.

      The jacket is *mine*.

      The gift is *yours*.

      The dog is *hers (his)*.

      Those bikes are *ours*.

      Take *your* turn before they take *theirs*.

# demonstrative pronoun

**The 4 demonstrative pronouns are: this, that, these, those.**

This baseball cap is mine.
(***This*** refers to an object close to you.)

These belong to Jim.
(***These*** refers to objects close to you.)

That is new.
(***That*** refers to an object away from you.)

Those are pretty.
(***Those*** refers to objects away from you.

## interrogative pronoun

***An interrogative pronoun is a pronoun used to ask a question.***

> **Which** of those is mine?
>
> **What** would you like to eat?
>
> **Who** are you?
>
> **Whose** books are these?
>
> To **whom** would you like to speak?

### indefinite pronoun

***An indefinite pronoun refers to people, places, and things without pointing to any specific one.***

*examples of indefinite pronouns:*

>all
>anybody
>anyone
>anything
>each
>everybody
>everyone
>no one
>some
>someone

*Indefinite pronouns that end in -one are always singular.* (<u>Everyone</u> <u>is</u> coming to the party.)

*Indefinite pronouns that end in -body are always singular.* (<u>Everybody</u> <u>loves</u> me.)

*The indefinite pronouns — both, few, many, others, several — are always plural.* (<u>Both</u> movies <u>are</u> good.)

*The indefinite pronouns — all, any, more, most, none, some — can be singular or plural, depending on how they are used.*

(Indefinite pronouns are also discussed in Chapter 4.)

## relative pronoun

***The relative pronouns are: that, which, whom, who, whose, whoever, whomever, whichever.***

*A relative pronoun —*

1. introduces a clause (a group of words containing a subject and a verb).
2. connects with (relates to) another part of the sentence.
3. modifies a word (describes it/makes it more specific).

All that sounds confusing, but the examples below illustrate that relative pronouns are pretty easy to spot.

The book that she recently read is part of a series.
**That** relates to "book" and introduces the clause, ***that she recently read***.

The flower, which is on the table, is pretty.
**Which** relates to "flower" and introduces the clause, ***which is on the table***.

The class is being taught by the teacher whom was hired last week.
**Whom** relates to "teacher" and introduces the clause, ***whom was hired last week***.

Pete, who is a lot of fun, went to the game with us.
**Who** relates to "Pete" and introduces the descriptive clause, ***who is a lot of fun***.

Whoever crosses the line first should be the winner.
**Whoever** relates to "winner" and introduces the clause, ***whoever crosses the line first***.

You may have whichever gift appeals to you.
**Whichever** relates to "gift" and introduces the clause, ***whichever gift appeals to you***.

When to use **who** and when to use **whom** can be confusing.

*(subject)* **Whoever** told you that was wrong.

*(object)* I will speak to **whomever** is available.

## ADJECTIVE

**An adjective is a word that describes a noun or pronoun.**

Adjectives give more details about nouns which make the nouns more interesting.

> *That is a beautiful dress.*
> (**Beautiful** is an adjective describing "dress.")
>
> *He is a good pitcher.*
> (**Good** is an adjective describing "pitcher.")
>
> *My mother painted the walls an ugly color.*
> (**Ugly** is an adjective describing "color.")
>
> *That is a **mean** dog.*
> (**Mean** is an adjective describing "dog.")
>
> She is *small* for her age.
> (**Small** is an adjective describing "she.")
>
> They are a *strange* group.)
> (**Strange** is an adjective describing "group.")

That woman in the **beautiful** dress may be a **good** person, but she has a **mean** dog.

## VERB

***A verb is a word that describes an action.***

He ***ran*** the marathon.

She ***chased*** the robber.

Dave ***jumped*** through the ring of fire.

Max ***ate*** the ice cream.

Mike ***looked*** at me and ***smiled***.

That man ***scares*** me.

I am skateboarding. "Skateboarding" is a verb because it is something I am doing. It is an action.

### helping or auxiliary verb

***A helping verb is also called an auxiliary verb.***

1. Helping verbs are words that help the action verb.
2. Helping verbs come before the action verb to give support.
3. Because it has no meaning by itself, an auxiliary verb or helping verb, cannot be the main verb in a sentence. *A helping verb only takes on meaning when it is combined with another verb.*

Charlie <u>may lose</u> that watch.

They <u>are building</u> a fort.

He <u>can survive</u> on his own.

I <u>could learn</u> from you.

I <u>did write</u> the report.

I <u>do work</u> hard.

Mary <u>can dance</u>.

Char <u>should dance</u>.

Sally <u>must dance</u>.

Mattie <u>has won</u> the race.

I <u>am watching</u> television.

Maggie <u>might laugh</u> at that.

They <u>were playing</u> Monopoly.

He <u>could jump</u> that fence easily.

Dave <u>was laughing</u> harder than I was.

Think of an auxiliary verb as Robin and the action verb as Batman. The auxiliary verb helps the verb just as Robin always helps Batman.

**\*Important Note:**
A verb may be a series of words as in "has been eating." If two or more words make up the verb, the last word is the main verb and the other words are helping verbs.

linking verb

***A linking verb does NOT express an action.***

<u>*Verbs express action.*</u>

<u>*Linking verbs do not express action.*</u>

1. Linking verbs link the subject of the sentence to another word.

2. A linking verb describes what someone is being.
   An action verb describes what someone is doing.

   > Dave looked happy. (linking verb)
   > Dave looked for his glasses. (action verb)

   > Mike felt sick. (linking verb)
   > Mike felt the bug crawl up his back. (action verb)

   > The hamburgers tasted good. (linking verb)
   > Charlie tasted the hamburgers and barked with joy. (action verbs)

3. Linking verbs connect the subject to a word or words that rename the subject or describe the subject.

4. The word following the linking verb is usually an adjective, noun, or pronoun.

   > Karel is my sister. (noun — renames subject)

   > It is I. (pronoun — renames subject)

   > The food tastes terrible. (adjective — describes subject)

### *Stanford's list of linking verbs*

| | |
|---|---|
| acted | is getting |
| am | look |
| appear | might be |
| are | proves |
| are being | remain |
| be | remains |
| became | seen |
| become | smell |
| been | sounds |
| being | turn |
| feel | was |
| grow | were |
| is | will be |

*(And that brings us to predicate nominatives and predicate adjectives which will be covered in the next few pages.)*

## predicate nominative, predicate adjective

***A predicate nominative renames the subject.***

***A predicate adjective provides information about the subject of the sentence.***

<u>A predicate nominative comes after a linking verb and renames the subject of the sentence.</u>

The predicate nominative and the subject of the sentence are interchangable. In other words, the sentence will still make sense if you switch the predicate nomintive and the subject. You can substitute the word "equals" for the verb without changing the meaning of the sentence.

*examples:*

David is my son. (*son* is the predicate nominative)

Michael is an attorney. (in this case, *attorney* is the predicate nominative. Michael = attorney)

Murphy is my dog. (*dog* is the predicate nominative. dog = Murphy)

## more about predicate adjectives and predicate nominatives

*The predicate adjective also follows a linking verb, but it describes or provides information about the subject.*

*examples:*

He is afraid of that clown. (The predicate adjective is *afraid*. It describes how "he" feels.)

My mother was proud of me. (***Proud*** is the predicate adjective describing my mother.)

That movie was awful . (The predicate adjective is ***awful*** decribing the movie.)

A single sentence can contain more than one predicate nominative or predicate adjective.

*examples of multiple predicate nominatives in one sentence:*

Lincoln was a good *man* and a fine *president*.
He is my *father* and my *coach*.
Dave is a *graphic designer* and a *genius*.

*examples of multiple predicate adjectives in one sentence:*

The air smells *fresh* and *clean*.
His bedroom is *dirty* and *stinky*.
I am *healthy* and *happy*.

A single sentence can also contain both a predicate nominative and a predicate adjective.

*example:*

Sandy is a teacher and is happy.
(The predicate nominative is ***teacher*** and ***happy*** is the predicate adjective.)

## ADVERB

***An adverb is a word that explains —
how? when? where? in what way? to what extent?***

He kicks the ball **well**. (how)

He ran **fast**. (how)

She visited **recently**. (when)

He responded **immediately**. (when)

Washington slept **here**. (where)

He put it **there**. (where)

Jim played the piano **expertly**. (in what way)

Jan looked at me **weirdly**. (in what way)

He was **extremely** happy. (to what extent)

He talked **enough** for both of us. (to what extent)

Adding "ly" to an adjective often turns the adjective into an adverb. So when trying to find adverbs in a sentence, look for words ending in "ly"

That's a *beautiful* dress. (adjective)
She dresses *beautifully*. (adverb)

> She is a *kind* person. (adjective)
> She spoke *kindly* of the old man. (adverb)

Bobby was a *restless* sleeper. (adjective)
Bobby slept *restlessly*. (adverb)

> We'll meet in the *near* future. (adjective)
> He *nearly* won the race. (adverb)

Elaine is a *happy* girl. (adjective)
Elaine talked *happily* for hours. (adverb)

> John was a *quiet* man. (adjective)
> John sat *quietly*. (adverb)

He seems like a *normal* boy. (adjective)
He is breathing *normally*. (adverb)

> This is a *real* problem. (adjective)
> Is she *really* going with them? (adverb)

Adding "ly" to an adjective often turns the adjective into an adverb.

So when trying to find adverbs in a sentence, look for words ending in "ly."

## PREPOSITION

**A preposition is a word that explains where something is located or when something happened.**

*Where something is located —*

> above
> below
> over
> under
> in

*When something happened —*

> through
> during
> after
> by
> until

The word or phrase that follows (is introduced by) the preposition is the object of the preposition.

*(Stanford can make prepositions a lot easier for you. Check out his helpful hints on the next page.)*

A preposition is anything a little mouse can do with three boxes. With very few exceptions, this rule holds true. (Just fill in the blank with any of the prepositions listed below.)

A mouse can go _____ the boxes.

across, against, along, about, among, around, at, atop, behind, beneath, beside, between, beyond, by, down, from, in, in front of, inside, into, near, off, on, onto, out, over, past, through, to, toward, under, underneath, up, upon, with, within, without

Of course, there are prepositions that are **exceptions to this rule**. They are: *but, until, than, as, like, during, of, except, since*. It is not as hard to remember the exceptions to the mouse rule if you realize the first letters of the words spell —

***BUT AL DOES!***

(41)

## *CONJUNCTION*

***There are three types of conjunctions of which you should be aware.***

        1. coordinating conjunctions

        2. subordinate conjunctions

        3. paired conjunctions

## coordinating conjunction

*A coordinating conjunction connects words in a sentence and connects equal clauses in a compound sentence.*

The coordinating conjunctions — *for, and, nor, but, or, yet, so* — are used to connect words for different reasons and to send different messages.

1. She must have been in a hurry, for she left quickly. (**For** connects two equal independent clauses.)
2. We are going to the rodeo and the movies. (**And** connects words or groups of words.)
3. He is not on the footballl team, nor is he on the baseball team. (**Nor** connects two equal clauses)
4. She said she likes me, but I don't believe her. (**But** connects two parts of a compound sentence to show opposite or different ideas.)
5. Should we play basketball or soccer? (**Or** connects words to express a choice or possibility.)
6. She is eighty years old, yet she still walks three miles a day. (**Yet** connects 2 independent clauses.)
7. I wanted to see the concert, so I ordered tickets. (**So** connects the clauses of a compound sentence to show a result.)

An easy way to remember the conjunctions is to remember they spell out the word **FANBOYS**.
For, And, Nor, But, Or, Yet, So

## subordinate conjunction

*A subordinate conjunction connects the unequal clauses (dependent clause and independent clause) in a complex sentence.*

*The subordinate conjunction is what keeps the dependent clause dependent on the more important main clause.*

### Stanford's list of common subordinate conjunctions

| | |
|---|---|
| after | since |
| although | so that |
| as | supposing |
| as if | than |
| as long as | that |
| as much as | though |
| as soon as | unless |
| as though | until |
| because | when |
| before | whenever |
| even | where |
| even if | where if |
| even though | wherever |
| if | whether |
| inasmuch | which |
| in order that | while |
| just as | who |
| now that | whoever |
| once | why |
| rather than | |

## paired conjunctions

***The paired conjunctions are:***

***either/or***

***neither/nor***

<u>Always use or with either.</u>

You must choose **either** the money **or** the prize.

The key was not found in **either** the garage **or** the shop.

<u>Always use nor with neither.</u>

The candy is **neither** sweet **nor** sour.

That snake is **neither** creepy **nor** slimy.

## INTERJECTION

*An interjection, also called an exclamation, is a word or group of words that expresses strong feeling.*

An interjection

— is not related to any other part of the sentence.

— expresses strong feeling or sudden emotion.

— is usually followed by an exclamation point.

— is short.

> Calm down!
>
> Hey! Stop that!
>
> Rats! I thought I had him fooled.
>
> Wow! That was cool!
>
> Hurray! We won!
>
> Awesome!

## ARTICLE

**An article is a word that defines a noun as specific or nonspecific.**

(Stanford believes *articles* are the *ninth part of speech*.)

The only three articles in the English language are the two indefinite articles — a and an — and the one definite article — the.

Articles are small words that can cause a lot of confusion if used incorrectly.

**A** and **an** are indefinite articles that are used with nonspecific nouns (person, place, or thing).

**A** and **an** are used when we do not know or do not care which thing is being discussed.

> Hand me a soccer ball.
> (By using "a" in the above sentence, you are asking to be handed any old soccer ball that is available.)

> Toss me an apple from the bowl.
> (By using "an" in the above sentence, you are asking for any apple in the bowl. You don't care which apple you get.)

*"a" and "an" are indefinite articles that refer to any old thing that is available.*

Both **a** and **an** mean *"one of something,"* but they are used with different nouns.

**A** is used before nouns that begin with a consonant (any letter that is NOT a vowel).

| a dog | a leg | a window |
|---|---|---|
| a plate | a cell phone | a text |
| a magazine | a cloud | a wish |

**AN** is used before words starting with a vowel (a, e, i, o, u).

| an animal | an elephant | an island |
|---|---|---|
| an ankle | an ice cube | an office |
| an egg | an ostrich | an uncle |

**The is a definite article. It refers to a "specific thing."**

*Hand me the soccer ball.*

(By using "the" in the above sentence, you are saying you want the specific soccer ball.)

*Let me look at the book.*

(By using "the" in the above sentence, you are asking to see a specific book.)

*Whenever you find an article in a sentence, you will also find the noun to which it is referring. Sometimes there is an adjective or adverb between the article and the noun.*

Please hand me the lucky stone.

    **The** is a **definite article** referring to a specific "stone."

    **Lucky** is just an adjective describing stone.

Try to kick a red ball to me.

    **A** is the **indefinite article** referring to "ball."

    **Red** is just an adjective describing ball.

# Chapter 3: Punctuation

*Punctuation is used to separate words so that sentences are easy to read and understand.*

The following are the six most commonly used punctuation marks.

        period

        question mark

        exclamation point

        quotation marks

        comma

        apostrophe

## PERIOD

***A period [ . ] is a punctuation mark used at the end of a sentence.***

> The dog ran home.
>
> I like apples.
>
> My father is a fireman.

Periods are also often used in abbreviations.

> Dr. Byron Cunningham
>
> 3:00 p.m.
>
> Washington, D.C.

## QUESTION MARK

**A question mark [ ? ] is a punctuation mark used at the end of a question.**

A question asks something.

>How old are you?

>Would you like a cookie?

>When is the circus coming to town?

## EXCLAMATION POINT

***An exclamation point [ ! ] is a punctuation mark used when strong feelings are being expressed.***

Exclamation points follow commands, very strong statements, and exclamations (expressions of surprise, anger, or pain).

>Ow! Don't do that!
>
>Stop! Stay where you are!
>
>Wow! That was cool!
>
>You are awesome!

An exclamatioin point follows statements expressing strong feelings or emotions.

## QUOTATION MARKS

**Quotation marks [ " " ] are always used in pairs to set off speech or a quotation.**

Use *quotation marks* with a **direct quotation**.
A **direct quotation** is someone's **exact words**.

Capitalize the first letter of a direct quotation when the quoted material is a complete sentence.

> "Go to bed!" his mother yelled.
>
> "Hello," said the lady. "What is your name?"
>
> She looked at him and said, "You are disgusting."
>
> My favorite Yogi Berra quote is, "When you come to a fork in the road, take it."

When a direct quotation is interrupted mid-sentence, do **NOT** capitalize the second part of the quotation.

> "I did not see a ghost," Mrs. Lawson said, "but I sure wish I had."
>
> "Take this food," said Mrs. Frank, "and give it to the homeless shelter."

**Note:** Do not forget to use quotation marks at the end of the quoted words as well as at the beginning.

(Stanford will explain <u>indirect quotations</u> on the next page.)

**Do NOT use quotation marks with an indirect quotation.**

An indirect quotation is what someone said but not the exact words used. Indirect quotations are *rephrasings* or *summaries* of someone's words.

Here are a couple of examples of indirect quotes requiring no quotation marks —

> Mr. Lawson reported that he saw a coyote in his back field.
>
> (These are not Mr. Lawson's exact words but an interpretation of what he said. In other words, it is what someone said Mr. Lawson said, so no quotation marks are neccessary.)
>
> John said he thought I looked beautiful.
>
> (Again, these are not the exact words John used but rather the speaker's interpretation or understanding of what John said. Therefore, no quotation marks are neccessary.)

*Here is a direct quote requiring quotation marks. Compare it to the indirect quotes above.*

> *Mr. Lawson said,* "The coyote looked at me and then vanished."
>
> *(These are Mr. Lawson's exact words, so they need to be set off with quotation marks. )*

## periods and commas with quotation marks

**_Periods & commas ALWAYS go inside the quotation marks._**
That's easy to remember.

    Janet said, "I want to go home."

"Harry," Mom said, "turn off the television and go outside to play."

"I will," he replied, "as soon as this program is over."

To get the door to open, just press the red button marked "Exit." (The word "Exit" is enclosed in quotation marks because it is the exact word that apears on the button.)

## question marks and exclamation points with quotation marks

***When it comes to using question marks and exclamation points with quotation marks, there are two rules:***

1. If the question mark or exclamation point is **part of the quotation itself**, the punctuation (question mark or exclamation point) ***goes inside the quotation marks***.

>I did finally get around to reading last week's assignment, "What Makes a Tree?"
>
>I asked you, "Where are you going?"
>
>He said, "Stop!"
>
>"Look at him!" she exclaimed. "What is he doing?"
>
>"What do you see?" he asked.
>
>The teacher asked, "Do you have your homework?"

2. If the question mark or exclamation point ***is part of the sentence as a whole (and not part of the actual quote)***, the punctuation ***goes outside the quotation marks***.

>Have you read the book, "Harry Potter and the Chamber of Secrets"?
>
>Do you agree with the saying, "If you can't say anything nice, don't say anything at all"?
>
>Who was it that said, "I will return"?

## COMMA

***A comma [ , ] is a punctuation mark used to separate a list of items, a list of activities, or a list of phrases.***

Use a comma to separate three of more items in a list.

    She likes to read poems, novels, and labels.

    Please go to the store for bananas, cereal, and milk.

    Bullying is mean, cowardly, and hurtful.

Use a comma to separate a list of three or more activities.

    He hit the ball, ran the bases, and crossed home plate.

    He called his sister, sent her an email, and drove to her home.

    It is important to be kind, considerate, and helpful to others.

Use commas in compound and complex sentences to separate clauses. (covered in Chapter 1).

## APOSTROPHE

***An apostrophe [ ' ] is a punctuation mark used to create contractions and possessive forms.***

*(Stanford will explain contractions first.)*

## apostrophes with contractions

***When you take two or more words and combine them into one word, you create a contraction.***

In creating a contraction, you always remove some letters from the words being combined.

In place of the missing letters, you use an apostrophe.

The apostrophe is used to show where letters have been left out of a contraction.

      do not (don't)
      I am (I'm)
      it is (it's)
      let us (let's)
      she is (she's)
      she will (she'll)
      she would (she'd)
      they had (they'd)
      who is (who's)
      would have (would've)
      you are (you're)

*(Apostrophes are also covered in Chapter 5.)*

## apostrophes with singular possessive nouns

***Possessive nouns show ownership or membership. He owns something, she owns something, they own something, or he, she, they belong to something.***

To show **singular possessive** (ownership) — add apostrophe + s [ 's ] to singular nouns.

    Jake's basketball *(By adding 's to the name Jake, we are saying that the basketball belongs to Jake.)*

    the Jones's house *(The house is owned by the Jones family.)*

    the child's book *(The book belongs to the child.)*

    Sara's bedroom *(The bedroom belongs to Sara.)*

    Bob's soccer team *(It is the soccer team on which Bob plays.)*

    my dad's car *(The car belongs to my dad.)*

    the man's golf clubs *(The golf clubs belong to the man.)*

If a word ends in "ss"

    Ross's football team *(Even if the name ends in **ss**, it is still correct to add 's to create the possessive form.)*

    Ross' football team *(It is also considered correct to add only an apostrophe to words ending in **ss**.)*

*(Check next page for suggestion by The New York Public Library)*

(The New York Public Library Guide suggests: "When a word ends in a double s, we are better off writing its possessive with only an apostrophe: the boss' memo, the witness' statement. Many writers insist, however, that we actually hear an "es" sound attached to the possessive forms of these words, so an apostrophe 's is appropriate: boss's memo, witness's statement. If the look of the three s's in a row doesn't bother you, use that construction.")

## apostrophes with plural possessive nouns

***To show plural possessive (ownership by more than one), make the noun plural first. Then use the apostrophe.***

>>the boys' game

>>the kids' toys

>>the dogs' bones

If a plural noun does NOT end in "s," add an apostrophe + s [ 's ] to create the possessive form.

>>the children's rooms

>>the men's golf clubs

>>the oxen's barn

## Chapter 4:
## Subject and Verb Agreement

***The subject of a sentence is the person, place, or thing that is doing something or being something.***

***The verb of a sentence describes the action being performed by the subject***

The verb must agree with the subject of the sentence.

  A *singular subject* must have a *singular verb*.
  A *plural subject* must have a *plural verb*.

Be sure the verb agrees with the *true* subject of the sentence which often is not the noun closest to it.

*(Stanford will help you with this in the next few pages.)*

1. The verb of the sentence must agree with the subject of the sentence.

   The dog is barking. *(singular subject, singular verb)*

   The dogs are barking. *(plural subject, plural verb)*

   The child is playing. *(singular subject, singular verb)*

   The children are playing. *(plural subject, plural verb)*

2. Ignore the words that come between the subject and the verb when deciding which verb to use.

   <u>The kittens in the box are cute.</u>

The subject is *kittens* (plural) so the verb must be plural. "*in the box*" is a *prepositional phrase*. If you take it out of the sentence, the sentence still makes sense. Therefore, it is ignored when determining the verb.

*(If you thought "box" was the subject, you would make the verb singular. The kittens in the box is cute. Sounds wrong, doesn't it? It sounds wrong because you are actually saying the box is cute. What you want to say is the kittens (subject of sentence)* **are** *cute.*

3. The subject usually comes before the verb in a sentence, but sometimes the verb comes before the subject. Just remember that whether the verb comes before or after the subject, the same rules for subject/verb agreement apply.

   <u>There are snacks for you on the kitchen table.</u>

   *(The subject is "snacks" (plural noun) so the verb (are) is plural.*

   <u>Where are they?</u>

   *(Subject is "they" (plural pronoun) so the verb (are) is plural.)*

   <u>There is a new book in the library.</u>

   *(Subject is "book" (singular noun) so the verb (is) is singular*

To double check if the verb is agreeing with the subject, remove the phrase (group of words) between the subject and the verb. If the sentence still makes sense, you know that grammatically you are doing the right thing.

Let's go back to our sentence again.

**The kittens in the box are cute.**

Take out the prepositional phrase, "in the box." Now your sentence reads, "The kittens (is, are) cute."

Your ear tells you clearly which is the correct verb to use. The subject, "kittens," is plural, so the verb must also be plural (are).

Here is another example.

**The kitten with the children is small.**

Even though the word "children" is plural, "is small" refers to the kitten so the verb is singular.

## verb agreement with indefinite pronouns

Sometimes indefinite pronouns (covered in Chapter 2) seem to be talking about more than one person. They look and sound like they are plural and should have a plural verb with them. Don't be fooled!

"-body," "-one," and "-thing" words are always singular because "body," "one," and "thing," are singular nouns.

### *examples of indefinite pronouns ending in -one, -body and -thing*

> anybody, anyone, anything, everybody, each, either, everyone, everything, neither, nobody, none, no one, nothing, somebody, someone, something

Indefinite pronouns that end in *-one* are always *singular* and need a verb that is singular.

**Everyone is** coming to the party.

**Someone was** here last night.

**Anyone is** eligible to win.

Indefinite pronouns that end in *-body* are always *singular* and need a verb that is singular.

**Everybody needs** to have the information.

**Anybody** with an interest in science **is** welcome.

**Somebody does not understand** the rules.

**Nobody likes** a bully.

Indefinite pronouns that end in *-thing* are always *singular* and need a verb that is singular.

**Everything looks** good.

**Something seems** to be wrong.

**Anything is** fine with me.

**verb agreement
with indefinite pronouns**

The indefinite pronouns - *both, few, many, others, several* - are always plural and must have a verb that is plural.

**Both perform** in the first act of the play.

**Few are** interested in participating in the game.

**Many feel** sick after eating the cafeteria food.

**Others have** already tried to open the safe.

**Several** months **have** passed since the argument.

The indefinite pronouns - *all, any, more, most, none, some* - can be singular or plural, depending on how they are used.

| | |
|---|---|
| Almost **all** of the food **is** gone. | (singular) |
| **All are** welcome in my home. | (plural) |
| **Any** dog here **is** adoptable. | (singular) |
| **Any** who want to attend **are** welcome. | (plural) |
| **Most** of the writing **is** done. | (singular) |
| **Most** of the kids **are** older than Jim. | (plural) |
| **None** of the horses **is** sick. | (singular) |
| **None** of us **are** happy about this. | (plural) |
| **Some** of my allowance **has** been spent. | (singular) |
| **Some** of the people **are** wearing costumes. | (plural) |

## Chapter 5:
## Capitalization

***The first letter of a capitalized word is upper case and the rest of the letters in the word are lower case.***

*Always* capitalize the first letter of the first word in a sentence.

*Always* capitalize the pronoun "I".

## All the following should be capitalized.

1. ***days of the week***
   Monday, Tuesday, Wednesday, Thursday, Friday, Saturday, Sunday

2. ***months of the year***
   January, February, March, April, May, June, July, August, September, October, November, December

3. ***first word in a quotation***

4. ***proper noun*** (*specific* person, place or thing)
   Abraham Lincoln was born at Sinking Springs Farm in Kentucky.

5. ***title used as a name or part of a name***
   Mayor Krueger, President Obama, Dr. Oz, Aunt Rose

6. ***initials***
   J. K. Rowling, A. A. Milne, John F. Kennedy

7. ***nicknames***
   Bubba, Junior, Champ

8. ***titles that clearly refer to only one person of high rank***
   President, Pope

9. ***family relationships when used in place of the actual name***
   I went to New York with Mom. ("Mom" is used as a substitute for her actual name so it must be capitalized.)

   Your mom is a nice lady. (If you try to substitute your mother's actual name in this instance, the sentence will not make sense.)

   Aunt Sophie came to visit. ("Aunt" is capitalized, because it is being used as part of the proper **noun**.)

10. ***races*** — Asian, Indian, Filipino, American Indian

## All the following should be capitalized.

11. ***languages***
    Italian, Spanish, English, French

12. ***holidays***
    Independence Day, Valentine's Day, Memorial Day, Thanksgiving Day

13. ***businesses and the names of their products***
    Lego, Hostess Twinkees, General Mills Cheerios

14. ***first word and last word along with all other words of importance in the title of a book, magazine, or story. Only capitalize articles (the, a, an) if they are the first word in the title. Otherwise, they should not be capitalized.***
    Gone with the Wind, The Tortoise and the Hare

15. ***national documents***
    Bill of Rights, Emancipation Proclamation, Constitution of the United States

16. ***names of stars and planets (earth, sun, and moon are exceptions to this rule and are not capitalized)***
    Mercury, Venus, Mars, Jupiter, Saturn, Neptune

17. ***historical events***
    Revolutionary War, Civil War, Industrial Revolution

18. ***specific places***
    Rocky Mountains, Australia, Oregon Aquarium,
    All continents are capitalized.
    All state names are capitalized.

19. ***America, American, United States of America, United States***

20. ***countries***
    France, England, Mexico, Italy, Germany

### All the following should be capitalized.

21. ***North, South, East, and West when used to designate specific areas.***
    Do NOT capitalize these words when they are used as compass directions.
       I live in the Pacific Northwest. (specific place)
       I like movies about the West. (specific area)
       Follow the road to the junction just north of Main Street. (direction so not capitalized)
       Do you want to walk north on the beach or south through town? (directions so not capitalized)

22. ***religions***
    Catholic, Baptist, Protestant, Jewish

23. ***nationalities***
    Swiss, Australian, Canadian, Dutch

24. ***titles that precede names but — not titles that follow names***
    Dr. Westmoreland
    Tom Westmoreland is a doctor.

    President Obama was first elected in 2008.
    Barack Obama was elected for a second term as president is 2012.

25. ***acronyms — abbreviations formed by the letters in phrases and organizational names.***
    FBI — acronym for Federal Bureau of Investigation.
    CIA — acronym for Central Intelligence Agency.
    omg — acronym for "oh my gosh."
    asap — acronym for "as soon as possible."

### Now let's look at words that should NOT be capitalized.

## Some words should *NOT* be capitalized.

1. ***trees***
    maple, oak, evergreen, spruce, poplar, birch

2. ***flowers***
    tulip, rose, pansy, sunflower, daffodil, carnation

3. ***diseases/illnesses***
    flu, tonsilitis, measles, mumps (Only capitalize a disease if it is named after someone.
    *Chrons disease, Hodgkins disease. Salmonellosis*

4. ***titles***
    following a pronoun or article
    *my dad, your mom, his uncle*

5. ***seasons***
    spring, summer, autumn, winter

6. ***directions***
    north, south, east, west, north of town, southerly winds, northerly squalls

7. ***school subjects***
    algebra, gym, history, social studies, science

8. ***breeds of animals***
    cocker spaniel, rainbow trout, collie, mutt
    (If the breed is referred to more specifically, some words may be capitalized - *English bulldog, Irish setter, German shepherd.*)

9. ***Capitalize the brand name, but do not capitalize the generic product's name.***
    Apple computer, Ford cars, Snickers candy bar, Wonder bread, Nike basketball shoes

## Chapter 6: Syllables

***All words contain at least one syllable.***

***All syllables contain at least one vowel — a, e, i, o, u, and sometimes y.***

A syllable is the smallest sound you can make when you speak.

***Words with one syllable have one single sound or beat.***

    house                dog

    game                mom

    ball                  pond

    frog                 tree

***Words with two syllables have two distinct beats to them.***

    monster (mon-ster)    garbage (gar-bage)

    doctor (doc-tor)        puppy (pup-py)

    roadway (road-way)   parrot (par-rot)

***Words with 3 syllables have 3 beats and so on and so on.***

    computer (com-pu-ter) 3 syllables

    complicated (com-pli-ca-ted) 4 syllables

    abracadabra (a-bra-ca-da-bra) 5 syllables

If you sing the Happy Birthday song slowly, you will clearly hear the beats of the syllables. Try it.

## dividing words into syllables

***Rules for dividing words into syllables:***

1. Divide the word between two consonants. A consonant is any letter that is not a vowel ( *a, e, i, o, u)*.

      happy  (hap-py)      basket  (bas-ket)

      dinner  (din-ner)      listen  (lis-ten)

2. Divide the word before a single middle consonant.

      honest (ho-nest)      table  (ta-ble)

      trouble  (trou-ble)      gleeful  (glee-ful)

3. Divide between words in a compound word. A compound word is a word made up of two or more other words. Compound words are covered in Chapter 7.

      birdhouse  (bird-house)      cowboy  (cow-boy)

      toothpick  (tooth-pick)      sidewalk  (side-walk)

bulldog  (bull-dog)

## fun facts about syllables

Sometimes when you make a word longer, you actually reduce the number of syllables.

Rugged (rug-ged) is a 2 syllable word.

If you add "sh" to the front of rugged, the word becomes a 1 syllable word, shrugged.

Here are examples of words going from 1 syllable to 3 syllables with the addition of just 1 letter.

Add an "a" to the end of "are" and it becomes a 3 syllable word, area. (ar-e-a).

Add an "a" to the front of "lein" and it becomes a 3 syllable word, alien (a-li-en).

### More Syllable Trivia Just for Fun

*Hotshot* (hot-shot) is a 2 syllable word that starts and ends with the same three letters. The word *restores* is another such word.

*Underground* (un-der-ground) is a 3 syllable word that begins and ends with the same 3 letters.

*Abracadabra* (ab-ra-ca-dab-ra) is a 5 syllable word that begins and ends with the same 4 letters.

## Chapter 7:
## Words, Words, and More Words

Compound Words

Contractions

Words Easily Confused

Onomatopoeias

Oxymorons

Palindromes/Anagrams

Synonyms/Antonyms

Words with Silent Letters

Fun, Useless Information (Long and Short Words)

## COMPOUND WORDS

***A compound word is a combination of two or more words.***

There are a limited number of words that can be made with the 26 letters of the English language.

By creating compound words, we add a lot more words to our vocabularies.

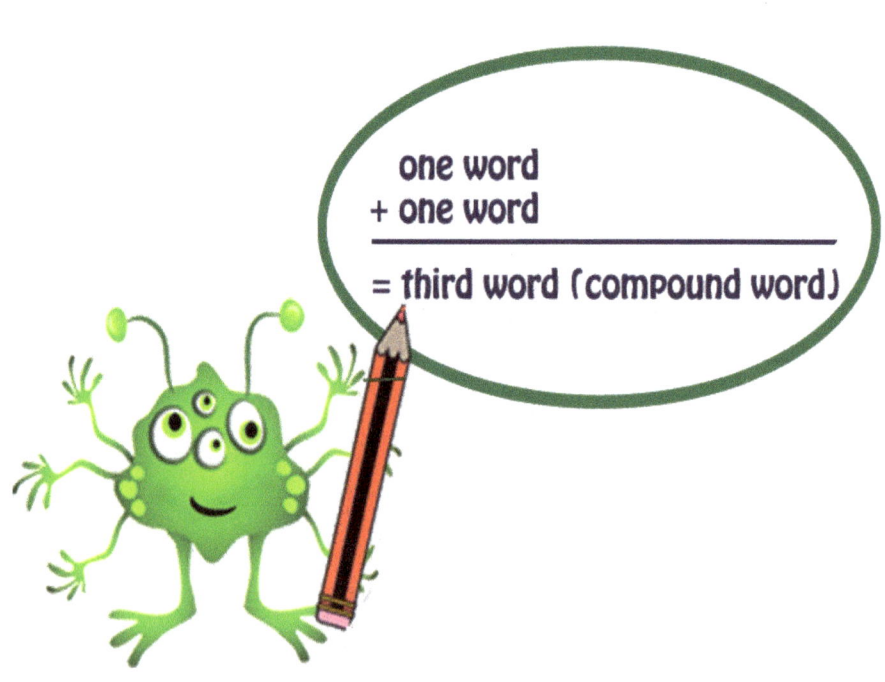

one word
+ one word
―――――――――
= third word (compound word)

## Stanford's List of Compound Words

**A -** airport, airtight, anyone, anytime, anyway, armpit
**B -** backstop, barnyard, Batman, bathroom, bedspread
**C -** catfish, clodhopper, congressman, cowboy, cupcake
**D -** dogcatcher, doorway, drawbridge, drawstring
**E -** earphone, earthquake, eavesdrop, earthworm, eyeball
**F -** farmhouse, fingerprint, fireman, football, fiddlesticks
**G -** gangplank, gatekeeper, gearshift, globetrotter
**H -** hailstone, hairbrush, handshake, homesick, haircut
**I -** income, indoors, input, inside, into, itself
**J -** jackass, jawbone, jaywalk, jackpot, jawbreaker
**K -** keyboard, keyword, kickoff, kidnap, kneecap
**L -** ladybug, landlord, landslide, lighthouse, lookout
**M -** madhouse, mailbox, masterpiece, merry-go-round
**N -** newborn, network, newspaper, notebook, nothing
**O -** outburst, outcome, outlaw, overgrown, overtake
**P -** peanut, pigpen, playpen, policeman, popcorn, potluck
**Q -** quarterback, quicksand, quartermaster, quickstep
**R -** racehorse, railroad, rainbow, rattlesnake, roadway
**S -** sandbox, scrapbook, shipwrecked, shirttail, sleepover
**T -** teammate, teardrop, thunderstorm, tiptoe, touchdown
**U -** username, undergrowth, upcoming, update, upload
**V -** viewpoint, vineyard, volleyball, voltmeter
**W -** waistline, wallpaper, warehouse, warpath, workshop
**X -** xylophone xenoblast
**Y -** yardstick, yearbook, yourself, yachtsman
**Z -** zigzag, ziplining, zookeeper, zooplankton

## CONTRACTIONS

***A contraction is a shortened version of two words.***

I + have = I've

# Stanford's List of Contractions

aren't (are not)
can't (cannot)
couldn't (could not)
didn't (did not)
doesn't (does not)
don't (do not)
hadn't (had not)
hasn't (has not)
haven't (have not)
he'd (he had, he would)
he'll (he will, he shall)
he's (he is, he has)
I'd (I had, I would)
I'll (I will, I shall)
I'm (I am)
I've (I have)
isn't (is not)
let's (let us)
mightn't (might not)
mustn't (must not)
shan't (shall not)
she'd (she had, she would)
she'll (she will, she shall)
she's (she is, she has)
shouldn't (should not)

there's (there is, there has)
they'd (they had, they would)
they'll (they will, they shall)
they're (they are)
they've (they have)
we'd (we had, we would)
we're (we are)
we've (we have)
weren't (were not)
what'll (what will, what shall)
what're (what are)
what's (what is, what has)
what've (what have)
where's (where is, where has)
who'd (who had, who would)
who'll (who will, who shall)
who're (who are)
who's (who is, who has)
who've (who have)
won't (will not)
wouldn't (would not)
you'd (you would, you had)
you'll (you will, you shall)
you're (you are)
you've (you have)

## WORDS EASILY CONFUSED

**It is very common for people to confuse the meanings of the following words:**

| | |
|---|---|
| accept, except | lead, led |
| advice, advise | like, as |
| affect, effect | look, watch, see |
| already, all ready | maybe, may be |
| anyone, any one | than, then |
| anyway, any way | their, there, they're |
| conscious, conscience | to, too, two |
| everyday, every day | were, we're |
| hear, listen | who, whom |
| its, it's | your, you're |
| lay, lie | |

*(Stanford is here to help!)*

accept, except

***Accept** is a verb.*

***Except** is a preposition.*

<u>***Accept** is a verb meaning "to receive or to agree."*</u>

>He accepted the trophy.

>He accepted her answer as truth.

>>*(a = agree or accept)*

<u>***Except** is a preposition meaning "all but."*</u>

>Everyone except Robert likes me.

>Mike likes every flavor except chocolate.

>>*(e = the exception of)*

advice, advise

***Advice** is a noun.*

***Advise** is a verb.*

<u>**Advice** is a noun. It is a recommendation, suggestion or idea.</u> *(The "c" is pronounced like an "s.")*

>If you are smart, you will take my *advice*.

>He gave me good *advice* about how to pick good friends.

>I took his *advice* and went home to cool off.

<u>**Advise** is a verb. It is the act of giving advice.</u>
*(The "s" is prounounced like a "z.")*

>Mom *advised* me that bullying could do a lot of damage.

>He *advised* me to try out for the team.

>My teacher *advised* me to try harder, so I took her *advice*.

affect, effect

**Affect is a verb.**

**Effect is a noun.**

<u>*Affect* is a verb meaning "to influence."</u>

>How will the new rules *affect* the team?

>How is owning a dog going to affect your life?

<u>*Effect* is a noun meaning "result or consequence."</u>

>I think the new rules will have a possitive *effect* on the team.

>The overall *effect* came as a surprise to us.

The letters in the word RAVEN might help you keep these two words straight:

Remember, Affect is a Verb and Effect is a Noun.

### already, all ready

***Already* is an adverb.**

***All ready* is an adjective.**

***Already* (one word) is an adverb expressing time.**

> She has already left for school.
>
> Is it two o'clock already?
>
> Her plane has already landed.

***All ready* (two words) is an adjective expressing complete preparedness.**

> He is all ready to go camping.
>
> She is all ready for the dance.
>
> Are you all ready to go on stage?

### anyone, any one

***Anyone is a pronoun.***

***Any one is an adjective plus a noun.***

<u>**Anyone** *(one word) is a pronoun meaning "any person" at all."*</u>

>Anyone with a brain could figure it out.
>
>That ball could belong to anyone.
>
>Does anyone remember his name?

<u>**Any one** *(two words) is an adjective + a noun meaning "an item in a group."*</u>

>Any one of the horses could win the race.
>
>Any one of those children can post the bulletin.
>
>Any one of you could be chosen.

## anyway, any way

***Anyway* is an adverb.**

***Any way* is an adjective plus a noun.**

**<u>*Anyway* (one word) is an adverb meaning "something happened or will happen in spite of something else."</u>**

>She was told to be quiet, but she spoke anyway.

>I told him not to cross the street, but he did anyway.

**<u>*Any way* (two words) is an adjective + a noun meaning "any direction."</u>**

>Any way we go, we will probably get lost.

>I will go any way except west.

**<u>*Any way* (two words) can also mean "any manner or any method."</u>**

>To get kids to do their homework, parents often bribe them any way they can.

>I will help any way possible.

It is never correct to use ***anyways*** (anyway with an s on the end) in speech or in writing.

## conscious, conscience

***Conscious** is an adjective.*

***Conscience** is a noun.*

***Conscious** is an adjective meaning "awake and aware."*

> Yesterday he was in a deep coma, but today he is conscious.
>
> He doesn't have a conscious thought in his head.
>
> Was that a conscious decision?

***Conscience** is a noun referring to the inner voice that is a "guide to good behavior."*

> Tommy's conscience would not let him cheat.
>
> She slept well due to her clear conscience.
>
> You can tell he has a guilty conscience.

## everyday, every day

***Everyday* is an adjective.**

***Every day* means each day.**

***Everyday* (one word) is an adjective describing something common or ordinary as in "everyday occurrence."**

Because it is an adjective, it needs to be followed by the noun it is describing.

>These are my everyday clothes.
>
>Soccer is an everyday activity.

Everyday (one word) is an adjective that must be followed by a noun it is describing.

### everyday, every day

<u>**Every day** (two words) means "each day." It is not describing anything so it does not need to have a noun following it.</u>

    I have to practice piano every day.

    I have basketball practice every day this week.

**Just remember:**

    *Everyday* always describes something so it must be followed by a noun.

    *Every day* can stand alone.

hear, listen

***Hearing** is something you cannot control.*

***Listening** is something you do on purpose.*

Even if you are not listening, you will hear sounds around you.

**Hearing** *is something you do without thinking.*

*If there is a noise, you hear it whether you want to or not.*

>John heard the garage door close.

>Sue heard her baby crying.

>I can hear the birds singing in the trees.

**Listening** *is something you work at doing.*

*It is an intentional activity.*

>I listened closely, but I still don't understand.

>Be sure to listen to the teacher today.

>I stopped *listening*, until I *heard* my name.

its, it's

***Its** is a possessive adjective showing ownership.*

***It's** is a contraction.*

***Its** is a possessive adjective.*

        The tree dropped its leaves.

        The kitten is playing with its toys

        The dog is too large for its kennel.

***It's** is a contraction for "it is."*

        It's a beautiful day.

        It's a big world out there.

        It's about time you got here.

lay, lie

**_Lay_ means "to put" or "to place."**

**_Lie_ means "to recline" or "to rest."**

<u>**_Lay_ means to place.**</u>
Lay is always followed by a direct object

>Lay the book down on the table.

>The chicken laid an egg.

>I don't like to lay the baby on the rug.

<u>**_Lie_ means to recline.**</u>
Lie does not require a direct object.

>I lie down when I take a nap.

>My dog likes to lie in the sun.

>He does nothing but lie around all day.

lead, led

**Lead is a noun.**

**Led is a verb.**

<u>**Lead** is a noun referring to a metal.</u>

>This is a lead pencil.
>
>She suffered from lead poisoning.
>
>The paint has lead in it.

<u>**Led** is a verb meaning to "guide or direct."</u>

>He led us through the forest.
>
>He led me to believe it was true.
>
>He led us on a wild goose chase.

### like, as

**Like is a preposition.**

**As is a conjunction.**

<u>**Like** is a preposition meaning "same."</u>

*Like compares one thing to another so it is always followed by a noun or pronoun.*

*Like is never followed by a verb.*

> He throws like a professional.
>
> He acts like a winner.
>
> She throws like a girl.
>
> She fights like a tiger.
>
> I look like my father.

<u>**As** is a conjunction meaning "in the manner."</u>

*As joins a clause (a clause always has a subject and a verb) to the rest of the sentence.*

*There are always at least two verbs in a sentence which uses the word "as."*

> She golfs as a professional would golf.
>
> He walks as a ninety year old man would walk.

## look, watch, see

**Look, Watch, and See are all verbs that relate to actions of the eye.**

**Look** *is an action verb. It is something you do intentionally but for a short amount of time.*

    Look at the shooting star.

    We looked in the attic for the old trunk.

    Do you want to look at the photograph I took?

**Watch** *is also an action verb. It is something you do intentionally but for a longer period of time.*

    Let's watch the parade.

    Watch where you are walking.

    I am going to watch the football game on TV.

**Seeing** *is something you do involuntarily. If your eyes are open, you see. You do it without thinking and cannot avoid doing it. You see whether you want to or not.*

    Did you see the shooting star?

    I saw the same shooting star that you did.

    I saw her steal the candy.

maybe, may be

***Maybe is an adverb.***

***May be is verb.***

<u>***Maybe*** *(one word) is an adverb meaning "perhaps."*</u>

    Maybe I should voice my opinion.

    Maybe I should leave for school.

    Maybe you should just be quiet.

<u>***May be*** *(two words) is a form of the verb "be."*</u>

    We may be in first place after this game.

    That may be your opinion, but it's not mine.

    That may be the smartest thing you've ever said.

than, then

**Than compares two things.**

**Then refers to time.**

<u>**Than** compares one thing to another.</u>

>She is smarter than I am.
>
>He is taller than she is.
>
>Mary is more active than I am.

<u>**Then** refers to a time other than now.</u>

>The circus will be in town then.
>
>We will be on vacation then.
>
>I will see you then.

## their, there, they're

***Their* is a possessive noun.**

***There* is an adverb.**

***They're* is a contraction.**

***Their* is a possessive noun. It expresses ownership.**

> I think they lost their dog.
>
> This is their house.

***There* is an adverb meaning "that place."**

> Meet me there at 2:00 this afternoon.
>
> I will be there as soon as I can.

***They're* is a contraction for "they are."**

> They're my two closest friends.
>
> They're the new students.

to, too, two

***To* is a preposition.**

***Too* is an adverb.**

***Two* is a number.**

<u>***To* is a preposition.**</u> *(Remember the little mouse with three boxes in Chapter 2?)*

>They came to school this morning.

>Are you coming to the party?

<u>***Too* means "very or also."**</u>

>She is too funny for words.

>They want to come along too.

<u>***Two* is the "number 2."**</u>

>He was born with only two toes.

>Our house sits on two acres of land.

were, we're

***Were* is a verb.**

***We're* is a contraction.**

<u>***Were* is the past tense form of the verb "be."**</u>

    They were just returning from the store.

    We were planning to do that.

    They were running a marathon at the time.

<u>***We're* is the contraction for "we are."**</u>

    We're glad you came for a visit.

    We're anxious to see you.

    Do you think we're in trouble?

who, whom

**Who is a subject.**

**Whom is an object.**

**Who** <u>is a subject</u> *(the word in the sentence that is doing something).*

**Whom** <u>is an object</u> *(the word in the sentence receiving what is being done).*

*(Many people have difficulty with who and whom so Stanford has a little trick that might help you.)*

Answer the question you are asking with "he" and then with "him" to see which sounds better.

If you can answer the question being asked with "him," then use "whom." (That's easy to remember. Both words end in "m.")

For example, if you are asking —

1. **Who** or **whom** is going to the store for me?
   The answer is, **He** is going to the store for me. (**Him** is going to the store sounds wrong.)

   There is no "m" in "he" so you know to use "who."(**He** is the person going to the store = subject)

2. Give it to **whomever** or **whoever** has earned it.
   In this example, the question is, **Who** should you give it to?" The answer is you should give it to **him**. *Him* ends in "m" so "whomever" is correct. (person receiving it is **him** = object)

**Your is a pronoun.**

**You're is a contraction.**

<u>**Your**</u> is a possessive pronoun expressing ownership.

>Your shirt is unbuttoned.

>Your words are confusing.

<u>**You're**</u> is a contraction for "you are."

>You're right about that.

>You're so smart.

When you are not sure whether you should use *your* or *you're* in a sentence, say the sentence in your head and see if "you are" makes sense. If "you are" does not make sense, use "your."

*example #1:*

We are going to see *your* teacher.
We are going to see *you are* teacher.

(We are going to see "you are" teacher does not make sense so "your" is correct in this instance.)

*example #2:*

*You're* going to be late for the movie.
*Your* going to be late for the movie.

("You are" going to be late for the movie makes sense so "you're" is correct in example #2.)

## SYNONYMS, ANTONYMS

**Synonyms are words that have the same meaning.**

**Antonyms are words with opposite meanings.**

To remember which is which, think "s" for same (synonym).

## Some of Stanford's Favorite Synonyms

fine/good
sad/gloomy
close/shut
handsome/good looking
trouble/difficulty
impolite/rude
speak/talk
top/peak
garbage/trash
funny/humorous
guide/lead

hard/tough
sincere/honest
loud/noisy
innocent/harmless
scrumptious/delicious
silly/foolish
center/middle
hurry/rush
hunger/starvation
gut/intestine
automobile/car

## Some of Stanford's Favorite Antonyms

after/before
all/none
always/never
asleep/awake
beautiful/ugly
behind/infront
below/above
best/worst
black/white
bright/dull
city/country
clever/foolish
closed/open
come/go

crooked/straight
cruel/kind
dark/light
day/night
dead/alive
dirty/clean
deep/shallow
early/late
easy/difficult
fat/skinny
intelligent/stupid
noisy/quiet
quick/slow
stranger/friend

## PALINDROMES, ANAGRAMS

**Palindromes are words, groups of words, or sentences that are spelled the same backward and forward.**

**Anagrams are words or phrases formed from the letters of other words or phrases.**

*(Stanford came up with quite a few.)*

(115)

### palindromes

**A palindrome is a word, group of words, or sentence that is spelled the same backward and forward.**

mom

dad

poop

ma'am

tot

race car

toot

pop

eye

deed

wow

Was it a cat I saw?

Was it Eliot's toilet I saw?

## anagrams

***An anagram is a word or phrase formed by reordering the letters of another word or phrase.***

    listen/silent

    snooze alarms/Alas! No more Z's.

    the earthquakes/that queer shake

    satin/stain

    march/charm

    Monday/dynamo

    earth/heart

    Mars/arms

    astronomers/no more stars

    the eyes/they see

    mummy/my mum

    Statue of Liberty/built to stay free

    astronomer/moon starer

    schoolmaster/the classroom

## SILENT LETTERS

***Shh! Words with silent letters are hiding in our midst.***

There are several reasons we have silent letters in the English language.

1. Many of our words are a combination of words and sounds taken from languages of other countries. For instance, the silent "K" in knife and knight comes from Old English which was spoken long ago in England.

2. Because many of our words come from different languages, some of them do not follow the rules of English pronunciation. I am sure you have heard that the United States is a melting pot. That is also true of our language. It is a combination of words from all over the world.

Bill Bryson, a successful author, described the frustration we have with the English language in his book, "From Mother Tongue."

"To be fair, English is full of booby traps for the unwary foreigner. Any language where the unassuming word fly signifies an annoying insect, a means of travel, and a critical part of a gentleman's apparel is clearly asking to be mangled."

## *examples of silent letters:*

***bt*** — The "b" is often silent as in debt, doubtful, and subtle. Yet in words like obtain or unobtrusive, the "b" is not silent.

***ch*** — Words starting with "ch" can have a "k" sound as in chorus, character, chemical. Yet in words like chance, choice, and choke, the "ch" is pronounced.

***gh*** — Sometimes the "g" is silent as in freight, daughter, though, right, and night. Other times the "g" is heard as in ghost, ghoul, ghetto, and ghastly.

***gn*** — When used at the beginning of a word, the "g" is silent as in gnome, gnaw, and gnu. The "g" is also often silent when "gn" appears at the end of a word as in sign, foreign, and resign.

***h*** — The letter "h" is silent in several situations.
  1. It is silent when preceded by a vowel at the end of a word as in cheetah, Sarah, and messiah.
  2. The "h" is silent after the letter "r" as in rhyme, rhubarb, and rhythm.
  3. The "h" is often silent after the letters "ex" as in exhausting and exhibition. Exhale is one exception to this rule.
  4. The "h" is silent in many words that begin with the letter "h" as in hour, honest, and honesty.

***kn*** — The "k" is silent as in knife, knock, and knee.

***l*** — The letter "l" is often silent when followed by the letters d, f, k, or m.

  (d) could, should, would

  (f) behalf, calf, half

  (k) folklore, chalk, stalk, talk, walk

  (m) psalm, salmon

***mb*** — The "b" is silent in many words including comb, lamb, plumber, and climb.

***mn*** — When "mn" appears at the end of a word, the "n" is silent as in autumn, and column.

***ps*** — When "ps" appears at the beginning of a word, the "p" is often silent as in psalm, pneumonia, psychiatry, and psychology.

***sc*** — When "sc" followed by an "e" or an "i" appears at the beginning of a word, the "c" is sometimes silent as in scene, scent, science, and scissors.

***t*** — The letter "t" is silent in many words including listen, castle, watch, and hatch.

***wr*** — When "wr" appears at the beginning of a word, the "w" is silent as in wrist, wrong, wrote, and wrangler.

***u*** — "U" is often silent when it follows "g" as in guest, guitar, tongue, guess, and guard.

*Silent letters sometimes tell us how to pronounce a word. The silent "e" at the end of a word like **bike** lets us know that the vowel that came before it, "i" in this case, has a long sound.*

## ONOMATOPOEIAS

Onomatopoeias and oxymorons are not the most important words in the English language, but they are MY favorite words. They are fun to know and fun to use.

***An onomatopoeia word imitates a noise or action.***

Onomatopoeia words are fun to say and fun to use. They imitate a sound, and their meaning is very clear.

***Onomatopoeia may be hard to say, but onomatopoeia words are easy to spot.***

The bee *buzzed* past me. (The word "buzzed" is a word which sounds like a bee flying, so it is an example of onomatopoeia.)

The fire *roared* and *crackled*. (The word "roared" and the word "crackled" are onomatopoeias. They imitate the actual sounds of the fire.)

# Ding, Dong, the witch is dead!

Sock, gush, kerplunk, squeek,
crash, whirr, hiss, purr,
mumble, hush, boom, crush,
click, zip, tinkle, chime, moan,
groan, cough, pop, crunch,
giggle, moo, vroom, oink,
zoom, pop, pow.

SPLASH!

**Clang, clang, clang went the trolley.**

## OXYMORONS

**An oxymoron is a combination of words with opposite meanings.**

An oxymoron is usually made up of two words that are opposite in their definitions.

These words are used together all the time even though together they make no sense. That is what makes them fun and funny.

An example of an oxymoron is *butt head*.

As your ear gets used to listening for oxymorons, you will be amazed at how often you hear them used. Stanford has a list of his favorite ones on the next page.

Oxymorons make no sense! That is why I like them.

## Some of Stanford's Favorite Oxymorons

| | |
|---|---|
| only choice | pretty ugly |
| act naturally | almost exactly |
| liquid gas | hot chili |
| freezer burn | silent alarm |
| minor crisis | alone together |
| seriously funny | friendly fire |
| crash landing | sweet sorrow |
| friendly argument | genuine fake |
| fine mess | bad luck |
| plastic silverware | bitter sweet |
| boneless ribs | buffalo wings |
| front end | hard water |
| wagon train | jumbo shrimp |
| long shorts | melted ice |
| necessary evil | safety hazard |
| small crowd | good grief |

**The word *oxymoron* is itself an oxymoron. It is a Greek term derived from "oxy" which means sharp and "morose" which means dull.**

## SHORT WORDS, LONG WORDS

This chapter will not help you in your quest to learn grammar, but the information is great to store away in your head for fun or to impress someone.

short words

***Some words in the English languare are very short.***
***I, you, me, to, if, it, as, so, at, be, do, he, no, we.***

These words might be little, but they are tough.

They are just as important and necessary as bigger, stronger words.

Now some fun, useless information:

The world's shortest poem is entitled Fleas:

> Fleas
> Adam
> Had 'em

The shortest word in the English language that contains the letters a, b, c, d, e, and f is *feedback*.

*Caesious* is the shortest word in the English language that contains all five main vowels in alphabetical order.

*Suoidea* is the shortest word that contains all five main vowels (a, e, i, o, u,) in reverse alphabetical order.

## long words

***Some words in the English language are very l-o-n-g.***

*Some say SMILES is the longest word in English because there is a "mile" between the first and last letters.*

*Honorificabilitudinitatibus*, meaning honorableness, is the only word Shakespeare used that was over 17 letters in length.

Lake Webster in Massachusetts has another name that is harder to spell and pronounce. It is probably the longest name in United States geography: *Chargogagogmanchargogagogcharbunagungamog.*

*Dermatogoyphics* and *uncopyrightable* (15 letters each) are the longest English words in which no letter appears more than once.

*Esophagographers*, on the other hand, is the longest word in which each letter occurs at least twice. In the word *sestettes*, each letter occurs three times.

*Aegilops*, which means goat grass, is the longest word in which letters are arranged in alphabetical order. *Spoonfed* is the longest word in which letters are arranged in reverse alphabetical order.

## Chapter 8: Grammar NO NOs

People form impressions of you by the way you speak and the words you use. That may not be fair, but it is true. It does not matter how smart you are, you will come across to others as uneducated or even stupid if you speak poorly.

*(Pay close attention to Stanfords rules)*
*on the following pages. They are very important.)*

## *What NOT to say under ANY circumstances!*

1. Do not say "ain't."

2. Do not say "Oh yeah?" or "Sez who?"

3. Do not say "Hey, you."

4. Do not use "nah" for no or "yeah" for yes.

5. Do not say "I could care less" when what you really mean is, I couldn't (could not) care less.

6. Do not forget to pronounce the "g" at the end of a word when you are speaking.

> Say nothing. (Do not say nothin'.)
> Say something. (Do not say somethin'.)
> Say going. (Do not say goin'.)
> Say listening. (Do not say listenin'.)
> Say doing. (Do not say doin'.)
> Say leaving. (Do not say leavin'.)

7. **NEVER** use a double negative — two negative words — in the same sentence. It is not only wrong to use a double negative, but it *sounds* terrible.

*examples of negative words:* **no, not, none, barely, nothing, nowhere, neither, nobody, no one, hardly**

> I didn't do anything. (correct)
> (Do not say, "I *didn't* do *nothing*.")
>
> I am not going anywhere. (correct)
> (Do not say, "I am *not* going *nowhere*.")
>
> I won't say anything about it. (correct)
> (Do not say, "I *won't* say *nothing* about it.")
>
> I don't have anywhere to go. (correct)
> (Do not say, "I *don't* have *nowhere* to go.")
>
> I don't want anything to do with it. (correct)
> (Do not say, "I *don't* want *nothing* to do with it.")

Now you are ready to take on the world, at least the English grammar part of the world.

Just keep this reference book close by in case you need reminders.

Good luck and remember, Grammar is not your Grampa's wife.

Your friend,
Stanford

www.ingramcontent.com/pod-product-compliance
Lightning Source LLC
Chambersburg PA
CBHW062022290426
44108CB00024B/2743